Animals I See at the Zoo

ALLIGATORS

by Kathleen Pohl
Reading consultant: Susan Nations, M.Ed., author/literacy coach/
consultant in literacy development

WEEKLY READER®
PUBLISHING

Please visit our web site at: www.garethstevens.com
For a free color catalog describing our list of high-quality
books, call 1-800-542-2595 (USA) or 1-800-387-3178 (Canada).
Our fax: 1-877-542-2596

Library of Congress Cataloging-in-Publication Data

Pohl, Kathleen.
    Alligators / Kathleen Pohl.
        p. cm. — (Animals I see at the zoo)
    Includes bibliographical references and index.
    ISBN-10: 0-8368-8217-2 (lib. bdg.)
    ISBN-13: 978-0-8368-8217-9 (lib. bdg.)
    ISBN-10: 0-8368-8224-5 (softcover)
    ISBN-13: 978-0-8368-8224-7 (softcover)
    1. Alligators—Juvenile literature.   I. Title.
   QL666.C925P63   2008
   597.98'4—dc22   2007006036

This edition first published in 2008 by
Weekly Reader® Books
An imprint of Gareth Stevens Publishing
1 Reader's Digest Road
Pleasantville, NY 10570-7000 USA

Copyright © 2008 by Gareth Stevens, Inc.

Editor: Dorothy L. Gibbs
Art direction: Tammy West
Graphic designer: Charlie Dahl
Photo research: Diane Laska-Swanke

Photo credits: Cover, p. 11 © Lynn M. Stone/naturepl.com; title, pp. 5, 9, 13 © James P. Rowan;
p. 7 © Ron Sanford/Photo Researchers, Inc.; p. 15 © E. R. Degginger/Photo Researchers, Inc.;
p. 17 © Barry Tessman/National Geographic Image Collection; p. 19 © W. Treat Davidson/Photo
Researchers, Inc.; p. 21 © Raymond Gehman/National Geographic Image Collection

Printed in the United States of America

CPSIA Compliance Information: Batch #CR217140GS: For further information contact Gareth Stevens, New York, New York at 1-800-542-2595.

Note to Educators and Parents

Reading is such an exciting adventure for young children! They are beginning to integrate their oral language skills with written language. To encourage children along the path to early literacy, books must be colorful, engaging, and interesting; they should invite the young reader to explore both the print and the pictures.

The *Animals I See at the Zoo* series is designed to help children read about the fascinating animals they might see at a zoo. In each book, young readers will learn interesting facts about the featured animal.

Each book is specially designed to support the young reader in the reading process. The familiar topics are appealing to young children and invite them to read — and re-read — again and again. The full-color photographs and enhanced text further support the student during the reading process.

In addition to serving as wonderful picture books in schools, libraries, homes, and other places where children learn to love reading, these books are specifically intended to be read within an instructional guided reading group. This small group setting allows beginning readers to work with a fluent adult model as they make meaning from the text. After children develop fluency with the text and content, the books can be read independently. Children and adults alike will find these books supportive, engaging, and fun!

— Susan Nations, M.Ed., author, literacy coach, and consultant in literacy development

I like to go to the zoo. I see **alligators** at the zoo.

"Gator" is short
for "alligator."
A gator has
sharp teeth!

Gators spend most of their time in water. They **swish** their long tails to swim.

tail

They swim after **prey** such as fish and turtles. A gator's strong **jaws** snap shut to catch prey.

fish

Gators have thick, bumpy skin. Their tough skin keeps them safe.

Sometimes, a gator looks like a long, bumpy log in the water!

On land, gators lie in the sun to warm up.

They walk on short legs. Their front feet have five toes. Their back feet have only four toes!

front feet

back feet

I like to see gators at the zoo. Do you?

Glossary

alligators — very big lizards that live in warm, freshwater lakes, rivers, and swamps

jaws — the bones that make an animal's mouth open and close

prey — animals that are hunted for food

swish — to move by sweeping from side to side

For More Information

Books

Berger, Melvin and Gilda. *Snap! A Book About Alligators and Crocodiles*. New York: Scholastic, 2002.

Richardson, Adele. *Alligators*. Mankato, Minnesota: Capstone Press, 2005.

Rockwell, Anne F. *Who Lives in an Alligator Hole?* New York: HarperCollins, 2006.

Web Site

Enchanted Learning: Alligator

www.enchantedlearning.com/subjects/ reptiles/alligator/coloring.shtml

Print an alligator to color and learn about the parts of its body.

Index

About the Author

Kathleen Pohl has written and edited many children's books, including animal tales, rhyming books, retold classics, and the forty-book series *Nature Close-Ups*. Most recently, she authored the Weekly Reader® leveled reader series *Let's Read About Animals* and *Where People Work*. She also served for many years as top editor of *Taste of Home* and *Country Woman* magazines. She and her husband, Bruce, share their home in the beautiful Wisconsin woods with six goats, a llama, and all kinds of wonderful woodland creatures.